I0161774

Foods and Culinary Utensils of the Ancients

Charles Martyn

Foods and Culinary Utensils of the Ancients

Copyright © 2020 Bibliotech Press
All rights reserved

The present edition is a reproduction of previous publication of this classic work. Minor typographical errors may have been corrected without note; however, for an authentic reading experience the spelling, punctuation, and capitalization have been retained from the original text.

ISBN: 978-1-63637-142-9

CONTENTS

CONTENTS

IN THE BEGINNING

The influence exerted by different foods over the physical and mental faculties of mankind is so marked as to verify the famous pun of the philosophic Feuerbach, "Der Mensch ist was er isst" (Man is what he eats). The advance of civilization has always been accompanied by an increased knowledge of culinary matters, until cooking has become a science and its various forms great in number. So in tracing back the history of foods, culinary utensils and their uses, we of necessity trace back the history of the world.

It is of course impossible at this late date to determine what was the first food of primeval man; ignorant as we are of even the approximate date of his first appearance and of the manner and means of that appearance.

But it is worthy of note that if he had not been endowed with an intelligence superior to that of the other inhabitants of the globe, his existence here would have been very brief. Nature provided him with a body which, in those days, was well nigh useless. His prehensile organs, his teeth, jaws, feet and nails, did not fit him for overcoming any of the difficulties entailed by the adoption of most foods prepared by nature. He could not tear his prey conveniently nor crack many nuts, nor grub roots, nor graze. His digestive viscera were in the middle age too bulky and heavy for the rapid movements of the carnivora; they were not long enough to extract nourishment from raw vegetables. The only foods, therefore, primarily obtainable by him which he could use to advantage were fruits and soft-shelled nuts.

As man, however, advanced in knowledge, his skill in the art of cooking rendered any or all objects used for nourishment by other mammalia fit subjects of diet for himself. This may appear a sweeping assertion, but the statements of reliable travelers prove its truth. The fact should be carefully considered by those who advocate a diet exclusively of vegetables, and by those few enthusiasts who preach that man was not "intended" to be a cooking animal.

Whatever else may be clouded with doubt, it is certain that man was so fashioned as to be compelled to eat in order to sustain life! In the beginning, instinct must have taught him that the consumption of food was the *sine qua non* of his existence.

When was the beginning?

The Biblical chronology of events prior to the Deluge is not accepted by scientists. The students of to-day believe, and seek to prove, that the earth has existed for several million years, and has passed through many different stages; that animal life was first evolved from the "inanimate" state of matter; that man is the most highly finished creature that has as yet been attained in the ascending scale of evolution, and that he will, in the natural course of events, make place for a still more nearly perfect being.

The exact date of the first appearance of man cannot now be ascertained. Geological research has led to the assertion that he probably existed thousands of years before the time usually assigned. But if we commence our history from the last great glacial visitation we find that the conceded date of its occurrence, about 5,000 years before the birth of Christ, coincides rather closely with the date of the creation as given in the book of Genesis. Assuming then that the neolithic, or stone age

2

followed not only the ice visitation, but the creation (to use a familiar phrase), the theory of many scientists and the story of the Bible agree on the one, to us, essential point—the birth of the first people.

Horace, in his third satire (first book), gives his views of the first food of the human race. (At that time, six hundred years before the Christian era, it was held that man was not created in a perfectly developed form, but was engendered from beings of a different kind.) He says: "When first these creatures crawled out of the ground, dumb and foul brutes, they fought for nuts, first with nails and fists, then with sticks, and later with weapons made of metal." This coincides with the deduction made in the third paragraph, that nuts have a just claim to the title of one of the "first foods."

These savages must have suffered from exposure to the occasional inclemency of the weather. To protect themselves, they, being endowed with an ever-increasing power of reason, resorted to the skins of wild animals for covering. Failing to obtain a sufficient number from the carcasses of those which had died a natural death, they conceived the idea of destroying life in order to obtain the coveted article. They may not at first have availed themselves of anything but the outer covering, leaving the flesh to be eaten by other animals or birds, but the flesh adhering to the hide would soon become offensive from decomposition, and what is more probable than that their common sense soon directed them to remove it directly after being stripped from the slaughtered animal? The teeth of the primitive man were constantly in use for many purposes; so, in tearing off the pieces of flesh with them, may the first appetite for meat as food have been acquired.

3

It is difficult to determine when food was first subjected to the influence of heat; it is still more useless to attempt to explain how the properties of fire were first discovered. It is presumed that the first fire witnessed by man, was caused by the fall of a meteorite, a volcanic eruption or a lightning flash. The observation of its peculiar effects excited the still dormant inventive spirit of the neolithic, and he essayed the production of it himself. Evidence proves that he first attained his end by striking pieces of flint against iron pyrites and letting the sparks fall upon some combustible material, placed accidentally or intentionally beneath. It is easy to imagine that it was soon learned that fire would destroy human life and that the pleasing odor of the burning flesh led to the use of cooked meat as food.

The cradle of the fathers of the human race was undoubtedly the southern portion of Asia. They were nomadic in their habits and satisfied their acquired cravings by hunting and fishing. The stone floors of the caves in which they made their temporary abodes were admirably suited to the building of their rude fires.

Ultimately these neolithics became owners of flocks and herds, usually of sheep and goats, and moved about from place to place in search of fresh pastures. Members of these flocks were slain from time to time as convenience dictated. When for any reason food was scarce, their other domestic animals, even their dogs, fell a prey to the insatiable appetite for blood. The forests abounded with living things, now generally classified under the title of "game," and these also contributed materially to the food supply.

No fancy methods of preparing meats or game were then practiced. Everything was either roasted or cooked by means of

4

hot stones. The roasting was in all probability accomplished by suspending the whole carcass of the animal, denuded of the skin, over burning embers, composed of the limbs of trees broken up into suitable lengths—as indeed do the gypsies of Europe to the present day. The roasted meat was at first separated from the body by the hand, later by sharpened sticks or flint flakes, subsequently by flint knives. There is no evidence of any metal being used for that purpose before the Deluge.

Though these first people are known to have partaken freely of the flesh of animals and of the fruits of trees, both of the nut and pulp varieties, there is nothing that leads one to believe that fish was used as an article of food until after the Deluge.

Turning again to the Scriptures, many interesting things may be noted. The first mention made of a flesh offering and of the ownership of domestic animals is in Genesis, when Abel "gave of the firstlings of his flocks and of the fat thereof," while Cain brought "of the fruits of the ground." The earliest mention of cooked animal flesh is found in Genesis 8: 21, when Noah offered up "burnt offerings of every clean beast and every clean fowl" after the Deluge. In the story of the creation, man is enjoined to sustain life by vegetable food: "Every herb bearing seed, which is upon the face of all the earth, and every tree in which is the fruit of a tree yielding seed" were given to him "for meat." Nothing was said about the flesh of animals. But, after the Flood, "God blessed Noah and his sons and said unto them: * * * Every moving thing that liveth shall be meat for you, even as the green herbs have I given you all things."

So in many ways scientists and the Bible agree on the habits of the neolithics. Both state that the primitive food of man consisted of nuts and fruits; both mention the subsequent possession of flocks and herds, and both refer to the knowledge obtained later of the effects of fire on meat—with the one difference that the evolutionists seek to prove that the meat so roasted was eaten, while the Biblical man prior to the Deluge offered it untouched to his Maker.

Although it is now generally acknowledged that the Deluge was not universal, it is undeniable that it marked an all-important epoch, for from it may be said to date the recorded history of the present race of men. From the posterity of Noah sprang up the principal nations which have made the world what it is to-day.

THE COMING OF THE NATIONS

If we accept the biblical chronology of the events which immediately followed the Deluge, we find that Noah and his three sons, Shem, Ham and Japheth, landed on Mt. Ararat and fixed their habitations in the plains directly below. A formal division of the earth into three portions was made by Noah about a hundred years later, when he was still in the prime of life and when men were beginning to multiply sufficiently to form colonies and settlements. One portion was assigned to each of his sons with his posterity.

The three territories may be roughly classed as the northern, or the region of the "ruddy men;" the central, the region of the "tawny men," and the southern, the region of the "blacks."

To the offspring of Japheth was allotted Garbia (the north)— Spain, France, the countries of the Greeks, Sclavonians,

Bulgarians and Armenians. The offspring of Shem were given the central region—Palestine, Syria, Assyria, Samaria, Babel or Babylonia, and Hedjaz (Arabia). The sons of Ham received the southern division—Teman (or Idumea), Africa, Nigritia, Egypt, Nubia, Ethiopia, Scindia and India.

Various causes scattered the posterities of the three brothers, and nations were founded in many parts of the world.

Ultimately six great monarchies were established, Chaldea, Assyria, Babylonia, Egypt, Media and Persia.

ASSYRIA AND OTHER KINGDOMS OF
THE TAWNY MEN

The territories ruled by Chaldea, Assyria and Babylonia were located almost entirely on the vast plains of Mesopotamia. Although (or rather because) these nations were continually at war with one another they may be considered, for present purposes, as one country.

Babylonia was the first to be settled, with Nimrod, the mighty hunter, as its monarch, about 2350 B. C.

Although Assyria advanced rather more in civilization than the other two, the constant warfare waged and the varying degrees of supremacy and subjection held by the three kingdoms necessarily resulted in much intermingling of their inhabitants and a consequent similarity of domestic manners and customs as they emerged from barbarism.

Agriculture soon became the most general industry. Wheat, barley, millet and sesame were largely raised. Other varieties of pulse and grains were plentiful also, as well as many excellent fruits, which have since been transported to our own countries with remarkable success.

The different grains were ground to varying degrees of fineness between two stones. The flour or meal was then moistened with water, kneaded in a dish or bowl, and either rolled into thin cakes or pressed by the hand into small balls or loaves.

The wheaten bread was generally preferred, but the poorer

classes were perforce content with the cakes of coarse millet or durrha flour, eaten with milk, butter, oil or the fat of animals.

Dates formed an important article of diet amongst the people of Chaldea and Babylonia, although they do not appear to have been very favorably regarded by the Assyrians. Date groves flourished in many parts of the land, and the fruit was dried and pressed into cakes. These with goats' milk and such vegetables as gourds, melons and cucumbers helped nourish the great mass of the population.

Other fruits, some of them found in great numbers, were pomegranates, grapes, citrons, pineapples, oranges, pears, apples and many small berries.

Bread, wine and a kind of honey were made from the fruit of the palm tree.

King Sennacherib called Assyria "A land of corn and wine, a land of bread and vineyards, a land of oil, olives and honey."

Nature seems indeed, to have blessed her first children with an abundance of the good things of life!

It does not appear that the flesh of domestic animals was eaten to any great extent, and the inference is that it was beyond the means of most persons, for when warriors, upon an expedition, were able to obtain it at the expense of others, they freely indulged their appetites. After their victories they killed and cut up sheep and oxen, and roasted the joints over the embers of a wood fire. Sometimes they boiled the joints or the whole body in a huge pot or caldron, over a dead wood fire—on which, also, pieces of the flesh were fried.

Amongst the upper classes mutton appears to have been the favorite meat. Chickens were also considered a great delicacy.

As the races of those days, with the exception probably of a few people closely confined in the cities, were great hunters, a plentiful supply of game was usually obtainable—venison, antelopes' flesh, hares, partridges, etc. The flesh of the wild boar was also eaten, but there is no evidence to prove that the animal was domesticated with the intention of using it for food.

According to Herodotus, some of the Babylonian tribes ate nothing but fish, dried in the sun, pounded in a mortar until the fibres would pass through a fine cloth, and then kneaded into a sort of bread and baked. At first a prejudice against this species of food seems to have existed, but later it was held in much esteem. The supply of both fresh and salt water fish was practically unlimited.

Locusts were also eaten with great gusto.

The culinary arrangements and operations are not yet very clearly defined by the chroniclers.

The fireplace, built presumably of well-burned bricks, was open at the top, about two feet in height, and occasionally covering an area of many square feet. Whether it was of square or cylindrical shape does not appear. Over the top was set or suspended a large bronze caldron.

These caldrons were sometimes of great value. They were usually circular in shape, flat or nearly flat at the bottom, without feet, and furnished at the rim with ears or rings to receive an arched handle or a hooked chain. Many belonging to

10

the wealthier classes were embossed with flowers and otherwise richly ornamented. They were commonly known as "seething pots." They varied from eighteen inches to five feet in height, and from two and a half to six feet in diameter.

Roasting was perhaps the most common mode of preparing meat, but it was also broiled, slices being cut from the divided joints and transfixed with wooden spits.

For delicate operations, a fire of coal was later on made in a portable brazier. The oven then used was cylindrical in form, much deeper than wide, and made of fire-burnt bricks or indurated clay.

In the houses of the wealthy, and the palaces of the monarchs, the cooks, though usually slaves, were treated with much respect. They were distinguished by the wearing of a cap (not unlike the tiara of the reigning sovereign, except that it was devoid of jewels and unsurmounted by an apex or peak), and they had numerous assistants to relieve them from all the menial labor.

The cook's knife, closely resembling the modern two-bladed dagger, was usually made of bronze, often thickly gilded, with a much ornamented hilt carved from the hard black wood of the Syrian terebinth. Some, however, were fashioned from bone, partly covered with metal and adorned with pins and studs of gold. Others had handles of ivory carved to represent the foreparts of bulls and other animals, and many were embellished with precious stones. Quite a number were of copper, with hollow handles.

Among the kitchen utensils was a jug with a long neck, an

angular handle, and a pointed bottom. It was usually suspended from a nail or hook.

There was also a plentiful and varied supply of vases, large and small, pitchers for holding water and other liquids, bowls, cups, pans, small bottles, ladles, jars and funnels—some of pottery and others of bronze, some of simple form and others elaborately patterned. The funnels were generally shaped like the wine strainers of to-day.

Skins were often used for holding both wine and water.

The dining tables were supported by props with one or several feet, in the houses of the rich made often of ivory and carved in the form of a lion or a hero such as Atlas, and among the poor of stone.

The plates and dishes were of stone, alabaster or bronze. The dishes were generally made with handles, either fixed or movable, by which they could be carried or hung on pegs when not in use, and the red unglazed basins bore inscriptions, in cursive character, running round the interior in many lines to the bottom.

The cups, especially those used for wine, were very beautiful. The lower part was often modeled in the form of a lion's head from which the cup itself rose in a graceful outward curve. Many of them were of gold and silver.

To Assyria is due the birth of the "culinary art" and its gradual growth to a state closely bordering on perfection. It will be noted that it was marked also by the manufacture of utensils and vessels far more costly and elaborate than any in use at the present time.

EGYPT AND THE EGYPTIANS

The recorded history of ancient Egypt which was, according to Herodotus, known as Thebes, commences with the reign of Menes, or Menas, who is supposed to have been its first king. He ascended the throne about 2320 B. C.

The growth of civilization among the early Egyptians was much more rapid than among the people of any contemporary nation. Even in the days of Abraham and Joseph they had attained to as high a degree of social culture as during the most glorious periods of their career. In art and science their advancement was especially marked.

In her infancy, Egypt contented herself with the pursuits of agriculture, the chase, and, as the habits of the people became more settled, the rearing of cattle.

The domestic oxen were usually of the hump-backed variety. But not only were the ordinary domestic animals tamed and reared, but also animals such as gazelles and oryxes.

Sheep, though, do not appear to have been generally eaten; in some parts it was, indeed, unlawful to devour them.

Goats were kept, presumably for their milk, and kids were occasionally allowed to browse on the vines in order to impart to their flesh a more delicate flavor.

Pigs were generally looked upon as unclean, and therefore unfit for food. The chroniclers show them as used for food at only one festival. Those represented on the monuments were ugly in the extreme, with long legs and necks, rough hair, and a crest of bristles running down the back.

Beef and goose were more generally eaten than any other kind of animal food. The flesh of the cow was, though, never consumed on account of its supposedly sacred character.

The animals chiefly hunted were the gazelle, wild goat, auk, wild ox, stag, wild sheep, hare, porcupine and even the hyena. The wild boar is not represented on the monuments, but it probably thrived in ancient Egypt, for the country was admirably suited to its habits, as is proved by its tenancy there at the present date.

In lower Egypt, people were in the habit of drying and salting birds of various kinds, such as geese, teal, quail, duck, and some of smaller size.

Pigeons were also very plentiful and were much liked, and many of the wading tribe, as for instance the ardea, were so highly esteemed as to have been considered choice offerings for the gods.

The greatest favorite, however, was the Vulpanser, known to us as the "Egyptian goose," which, with some others of the same genus, was caught alive and tamed. They were also taken in a wild state to the poulterers' shops to be displayed for immediate sale, and when not so disposed of were then often salted and potted in earthenware jars.

According to Diodorus, the eggs of domestic birds were hatched by the use of artificial heat furnished by manure.

Of the wild birds, the "sic sac," a small plover, was often mentioned.

The river of Egypt was noted for the excellent quality of its fish (eaten both fresh and salted or dried), many varieties of which seem to have been peculiar to it. "The Israelites remembered with regret the fish which they did eat in Egypt freely."

The kinds most highly regarded were the oxyrhynchus, lepidotus and lotus.

The oxyrhynchus is now believed to have been the *mormyrus* or the "mizdeh" of the Arabs. It has a smooth skin and a long nose, pointed downwards. In some districts it was held sacred to Athor.

The lepidotus may have been the *salmo dentex* or the binny (*Cyprinis lepidotus*). As its name implies, its body was covered with long scales. Its flesh was excellent.

The lotus, sacred in the region of Latopolis, is supposed by De Pauw to be the *perca nilotica*.

Other varieties much liked were: The oulti, to modern palates the best of all; the nefareh or Nile salmon, which occasionally attained the weight of one hundred pounds; the sagbosa, a kind of herring; a species of mullet, the shall, shilbeh byad, kilbel bahr, (the Nile dogfish) a species of carp, eels, and turtles of the soft-shelled variety.

Eels were, though, considered unwholesome in summer (Ibid.).

Crocodiles were considered sacred in the neighborhood of Lake Moeris and of Thebes, but were eaten by the natives of the southern frontier.

The many restrictions imposed by religion and custom on the

15

diet of the early Egyptians subjected them to much ridicule from the inhabitants of contemporary nations, especially from the Greeks. Anaxandrides taunted them in his verses.

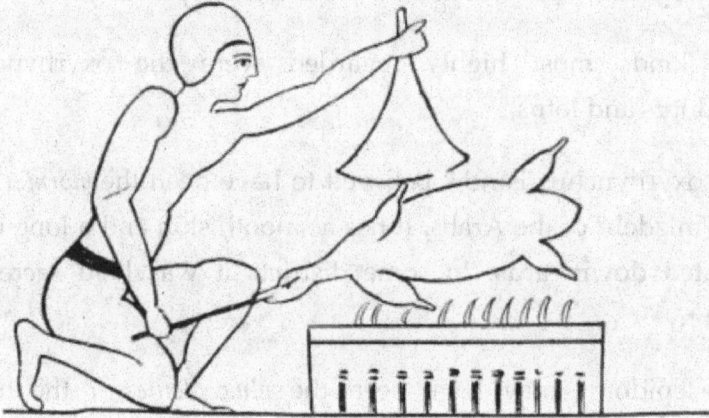

**Roasting a goose over a fire of peculiar construction
(From a tomb at Thebes)**

The priests lived solely on oxen, geese, wine, bread and a few vegetables. Mutton, pork and fish were expressly forbidden them. They were also warned to abstain from beans, peas, lentils, onions, garlic and leeks. On fast days they ate only bread and drank only water.

The people of the higher classes probably ate only two meals a day, as was the custom with the early Greeks and Romans. The breakfast was usually served at 10 or 11 a. m., and the dinner or supper in the evening.

In the early ages, before men had acquired the art of smelting ore, many of the culinary utensils of the Egyptians were either of stone or earthenware.

Knives were made of flint or stone, and were of two kinds, one broad and flat, the other narrow and pointed.

The skins of the goat and gazelle were fashioned into vessels for the carrying of water, and pans, dishes and vases for kitchen purposes were made of a red ware—sometimes of a light or yellow tint, sometimes of a brilliant and polished appearance.

The Egyptians were acquainted with the use of glass at least as early as the reign of Sesortasen II. (more than 3800 years ago), and made for it bottles and other utensils. Some of the former were made from two thicknesses of glass, enclosing between them bands of gold, alternating with a set of blue, green or other color.

As the Egyptians advanced in social culture, the wealthier classes gave more and more attention to the pleasures of the table. Banquets became more general and increasingly more elaborate. The sums of money spent on some of these entertainments were fabulous; they have never since been equalled in their costly, wasteful magnificence.

The preparation of a big dinner was in those days a weighty undertaking, for there were no big hotels to take the burden off the host's shoulders. Game had to be procured, professionals engaged, extra attendants hired, etc.

As all the meat used was freshly slaughtered, the kitchen and the butcher's department presented an active appearance for many hours previous to the feast.

In slaughtering, it was customary to take the ox or other animal into a courtyard near the house, tie its legs together and throw it to the ground, to be held in that position by one or more persons while the butcher prepared to cut its throat, as nearly as possible from one ear to the other, sometimes continuing the opening downwards along the neck, the blood being received in a vase or basin to be utilized later in cooking. The head was then taken off and the animal skinned, the operators beginning with the leg and neck. The first joint removed was the right foreleg or shoulder, the other parts following in succession according to convenience. One of their most remarkable joints, still seen in Egypt (although nowhere else) was cut from the leg and consisted of the flesh covering the tibia, whose two extremities projected slightly beyond it, as seen in the illustration.

The Tibia, a peculiar Egyptian joint

Servants carried the joints to the kitchen on wooden trays. There they were washed and prepared for the different processes of cooking. Then the various cooks were kept busy scouring the utensils, attending to the boiling, roasting, etc., pounding spice, making macaroni and performing all the other details of kitchen work.

The head of the animal was usually given away in return for

extra services, such as the holding of the guests' sticks, but it was occasionally eaten by the people of the higher classes, the assertion of Herodotus to the contrary notwithstanding.

Geese and other tame and wild fowl were served up entire, and fish also came to table deprived of only the tails and fins.

Vegetables were cooked in enormous quantities.

Bronze caldrons of various sizes were used for boiling. They were placed over the fire on metal stands or tripods or supported on stones. Some of the smaller vessels, used for stewing meats, were heated over pans of charcoal. They resembled almost exactly the *magoor* of modern Egypt.

The mortars used for the pounding of spices were made of hard stone and the pestles of metal.

Most of the bowls, ewers, jugs, buckets, basins, vases and ladles used in the kitchen were made of bronze alloyed with tin and iron. The usual proportion of tin was 12 per cent. and iron 1 per cent., although occasionally the amount of tin was as high as 15 (Ibid.) and as low as 6 per cent.

Slaves boiling meat and stirring fire

Simpula, or ladles, were commonly made of bronze (often gilded), with the curved summit of the handle, which served to suspend the ladle at the side of the tureen or other vessel, terminating in the likeness of a goose's head (a favorite Egyptian ornament).

Small strainers or collanders of bronze were also used, though for kitchen purposes they were made of strong papyrus stalks or rushes.

The spoons were of various forms and made from ivory, wood and divers metals. In some the handle ended in a hook, by which when required they were suspended on nails. The handles of others were made to represent men, women or animals. Many were ornamented with lotus flowers.

Skins were also used for holding wine and water.

The roasting was performed over fire burning in shallow pans. These were regulated by slaves, who raised them with pokers and blew them with bellows worked by the feet.

Though the Egyptians, except when impelled by the desire for extravagant display, partook sparingly of all but one or two meats, they were fond of a great variety of cakes and dainty confections. The more elaborate forms of pastry were mixed with fruits and spirits, and shaped to represent animals, birds and human beings.

The plainer rolls were generally mixed and shaped by hand and sprinkled with seeds before baking. At other times, though, they were prepared from a thinner mixture, first well kneaded in a large wooden bowl (the feet often being used for this purpose), and then carried in vases to the chief pastry cook, who formed it into a sort of macaroni upon a metal pan over the fire, stirring the mixture with a wooden spatula, whilst an assistant stood ready with two pointed sticks to remove it when sufficiently cooked.

Wine and water were placed in porous jars and fanned until cool. The water was purified by the use of paste of almonds (as it is, indeed, at the present day).

In the meantime, the reception room had been arranged for the guests. Chairs or stools were placed in rows or groups, extra carpets and mats strewn about, flowers put in and around vases and the house decorated in every other conceivable manner.

When guests began to arrive, they were first received in the vestibule by the attendants, who presented them with bouquets, placed garlands of lotus upon their heads and sometimes collars of lotus around their necks. To those who had come from a distance, they offered water and rinsed their feet. They then anointed their heads with sweet-smelling unguents and offered them wine and other beverages. During these proceedings the visitors were generally seated on the mats.

After having received these attentions, the ladies and gentlemen intermingled and passed on to the main apartment, where the host and hostess received them and begged them to take their seats on the chairs and fauteuils which had been arranged for them. Here more refreshments were handed around and more flowers offered, while the guests, generally in couples, but sometimes in groups, conversed with one another. Music was next commonly introduced, sometimes accompanied by dancing. The performers in both acts were professionals and the

21

dancing girls nearly if not quite naked. Sometimes at the same party there would be two bands, which we may suppose played alternately. Pet animals, such as dogs, gazelles and monkeys, were also often present (Ibid.).

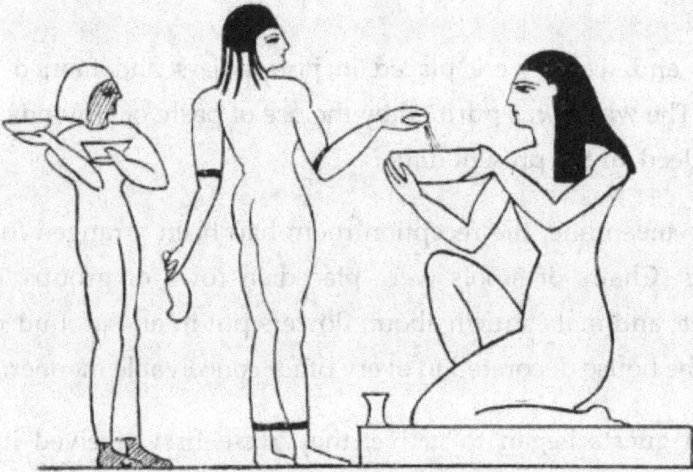

A black and white slave waiting upon a lady

On some occasions the music, dancing and light refreshments constituted the whole of the entertainment, but more generally the proceedings described formed only the prelude to the more important part to follow. The stone pictures show us round tables loaded with a great variety of delicacies, such as joints of meat, geese, duck and waterfowl of different kinds, cakes, pastry, fruits, etc., interspersed amongst the guests.

These tables could be more accurately described as low stools supporting round trays. The stool or pillar was often in the shape of a man, usually a captive, who bore the slab on his head. The whole was made of stone or some hard wood. It was not often covered with linen, but was from time to time cleansed with a moist rag or cloth (Homer).

The dishes were probably handed round by the attendants and the guests helped themselves with their hands, as knives and forks were then unknown and the spoons that were manufactured do not seem to have been used for eating. The guests took as much as they could hold in their hands and, after eating, dipped them in water or wiped them in napkins which, it will be observed, the waiters carried. Beer and wine were supplied to quench the thirst.

As individual cups were not usually seen, the women were presented with the desired beverage in silver vases, and the men with it in hand goblets, which after being drained were returned to the attendant. Women and men both imbibed freely and drunkenness was a universal and fashionable habit of both sexes.

When the country was in the zenith of her power and magnificence, the drinking goblets were of gold, silver, glass, porcelain, alabaster and bronze. They varied also in form, some plain in appearance, others beautifully engraved and studded with precious stones. Heads of animals often adorned the handles, the eyes frequently composed of various gems. Many were without handles, while others were so shaped as to more properly come under the name of beakers and saucers. The beakers were frequently made of alabaster with a round base, which prevented their maintaining an upright position without additional support; and when empty they were turned downwards upon their rims. The saucers, which were of glazed pottery, were ornamented with lotus and fish carved or molded on their concave surface.

Many of the vases have never yet been surpassed in daintiness of ornamentation. The most remarkable were those fashioned from porcelain which was made of a fine sand or grit, loosely fused and covered with a thick silicious glaze of a blue, green, white, purple or yellow color. The blue tints obtained have never been equalled in modern times.

Herodotus tells us that, after the heavier part of a banquet, it was the custom to have a man carry round a coffin containing a wooden image in exact imitation of a corpse. Showing this to each of the revelers, the bearer would say: "Look upon this and then drink and enjoy yourself, for when dead you will be like unto this." A rather weird observance, which might be traced back to the death of Osiris.

If the phrases are correctly reported, we must suppose the figure, brought in after the eating was ended and when the drinking began, was for the purpose of stimulating the guests to still greater conviviality. But if that were the case when Herodotus visited Egypt it must have been originated with a very different intention. The Egyptians were too much inclined to excesses in eating and drinking, both men and women (Herodotus and Plutarch), and the priests probably endeavored to thus check their too riotous mirth without personally interfering. Plutarch said concerning it:

"The skeleton which the Egyptians appropriately introduce at their banquets, exhorting the guests to remember that they shall soon be like him, though he comes as an unwelcome and unseasonable boon companion, is nevertheless in a certain degree seasonable, if he exhorts them not to drink too deeply or indulge only in pleasures, but to cultivate mutual friendship and affection and not to render life, which is short in duration, long by evil deeds."

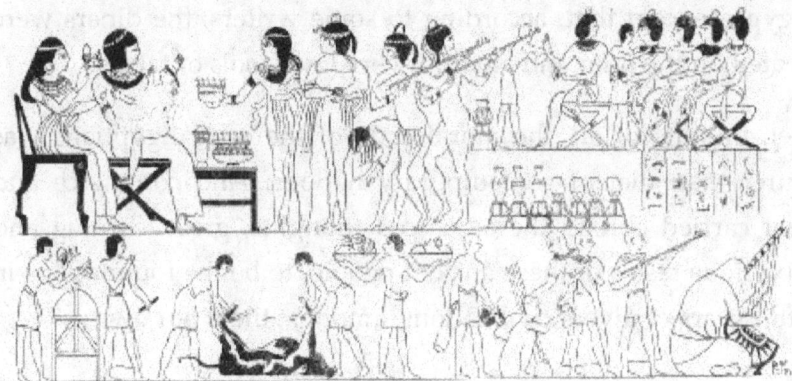

EGYPTIAN PARTY (From a Tomb at Thebes)

Host and hostess receiving presents. Dancing girls. Slaves
waiting on guests. Placing collars of lotus around their necks.
Slaves preparing bouquets. Scribe. Butchers cutting up ox.
Carrying trays of meat. Man clapping hands and singing.
Guitar player. Harpist. Slave carrying head and haunch.
Stick custodian rewarded.

After the skeleton, there was sung a doleful song in honor of
Maneros, whose identity is clouded by traditional disputes.

Next, music and songs of more mirthful character were resumed.
Sometimes jugglers, male and female, were hired for the
occasion. They amused their audience with ball tossing, turning
somersaults, leaping and wrestling. Occasionally, games,
resembling our draughts or checkers, served to amuse those
present (Ibid.), but as a rule the fumes of wine prevented any
such quiet occupation, and the festival in many cases ended with
a most riotous carousal.

The foregoing is probably a true picture of a banquet in ancient

Egypt—except that, according to some writers, the diners were seated on the floor and ate from very low stools or tables.

Yet, in spite of all, the moral code of the early Egyptians was purer than that of contemporary nations. And commerce and war carried abroad the advanced thoughts, great learning and luxurious tastes of these ancient people, to be the foundations in after years of divers civilizations, amongst them our own.

THE "VEGETABLE KINGDOM" OF ANCIENT EGYPT

The vegetable kingdom of ancient Egypt may be roughly divided into four great classes—trees and shrubs, esculent plants, grains and artificial grasses.

Of the first named, the most important food providing trees were the doom and date palms, the sycamore, tamarisk and mokhayp or *myxa*.

The doom palm (*Cucifera Thebaica*) grows abundantly throughout all upper Egypt. It is a very picturesque tree which, unlike its date-bearing sister, spreads out into numerous limbs or branches, reaching an elevation of about thirty feet. Its wood is more solid than that of the date tree, and was found to be very serviceable for the building of boats, etc.

The blossoms are of two kinds, male and female. The fruit, which is developed from the female blossom, grows in large clusters, each fruit attaining the size of a goose's egg, although the nut within the fibrous external envelope is not much bigger than a large almond. The flavor of the nut is peculiarly sweet, resembling our ginger bread. It was eaten both in a ripe and unripe condition—in the latter it has about the texture of cartilage; in the former it is harder, and has been compared to the edible portion of the cocoanut.

The date palm is too well known to need any general description. Two kinds, however, flourished—the wild and the cultivated. The wild variety grew from seeds, and often bore an enormous quantity of fruit. Sir G. Wilkinson is authority for the statement that a single bunch has been known to contain between 6,000 and 7,000 dates, and as it is a common thing for a tree to bear from five to twenty-two bunches, the average total is often from 30,000 to 100,000 dates per tree. The fruit is, though, small and of poor quality, and consequently it is not often gathered.

The cultivated variety was grown from off-shoots selected with care, planted out at regular intervals and abundantly irrigated (Ibid.). It began to bear in five or six years and continued productive for sixty or seventy.

Besides the amount of nourishing food furnished and the value of the wood of the date palm, an exhilarating drink was made from its sap and brandy or *lowbgeh*, date wine and vinegar from the fruit without much difficulty.

The fruit of the sycamore (*Ficus sycamorus*) ripens in June. Although it was much esteemed by the ancients, it has been denounced by moderns as insipid.

The mokhayt (*Cardia myxa*) grows to the height of about thirty feet, commencing to branch out at a distance of twelve feet from the ground, with a diameter at the base of about three feet. Its fruit is of a pale yellow color, inclosed in two skins. Its texture is viscous and its taste not very agreeable. It was used extensively as a medicine, and was also, according to Pliny, made into a fermented liquor ("Ex myxis in Aegypto et vina fiunt").

Among other fruit trees and shrubs may be mentioned the fig, pomegranate, vine, olive, peach, pear, plum, apple, carob or locust (*Ceratonia siliqua*), persea, palma, christi or castor oil plant, nebk (*Rhamnus Nabeca*), and the prickly pear or *shok*.

28

The persea (*Balanite Aegyptiaca*) is a bushy tree or shrub which under favorable circumstances reaches an altitude of eighteen or twenty feet. Its bark is of whitish color, its branches gracefully curved, its foliage of an ashy gray hue. Its lower branches are supplied with long thorns; on its upper branches grows the fruit, which resembles a small date in general character. Its exterior consists of a pulpy substance of subacid flavor; its stone is large for the size of the fruit, and incloses a kernel of yellowish-white color and an oily, rather bitter flavor. Both the exterior and the kernel were eaten.

The nebk or *sidr* is another fruit of the date variety. It was eaten raw, or the flesh, detached from the stone, was dried in the sun. It enjoyed the reputation of being a sustaining as well as agreeable article.

The most common fig was that known to the Romans as "cottana," and by the modern Arabs as "qottaya."

The olives grown were large and fleshy, but contained little oil.

Vines were undoubtedly much cultivated, in spite of the assertion of Herodotus to the contrary. The bunches of grapes, when intended for immediate consumption, were, after being gathered, placed in flat open baskets. When intended for the wine press they were closely packed in deep baskets or hampers, which were carried to the shed or storehouse on men's heads or by means of shoulder yokes. The juice was extracted by treading or squeezing in a bag.

The juice of the grape was sometimes drunk in its fresh condition (Genesis), but fermentation was usually awaited, and the wine was then stored away in vases or amphorae of elegant shape, closed with stoppers and hermetically sealed with moist clay, pitch, gypsum or other similar substances.

The best brands came from Anthylla (Athenaeus), Marestis (Pliny and Strabo), and the tract about Lake Marea. Sebennytic, Thebaid and Coptos also produced light, wholesome wines.

The esculent plants consisted of both wild and cultivated varieties. Those most in demand were the byblus or papyrus, the Nymphaea lotus, lotus coerulea and the Nymphaea nelumbo (called by Pliny "colocasia" and also "cyamon").

The papyrus grew luxuriantly in ancient Egypt, especially in the marshy districts of the Delta, although it is no longer found in the country. The pith of the upper and middle portions of the tall, smooth, triangular-shaped reed was used for paper, but that of the lower portion and the root were regarded as an edible delicacy. According to Herodotus, it was prepared for the table by being baked in a closed vessel.

The Nymphaea lotus, which resembles our white water lily, was also a product of the lowlands. The seed vessels were collected and dried, to be afterward crushed and made into cakes. The rest of the plant was also eaten cooked or raw, and was said to be of a "pleasant sweet taste," but nineteenth century palates declare it to be no better than a bad truffle. The lotus coerulea was merely another variety of the same plant.

The Nymphaea nelumbo, which is, by the way, no longer found in Africa, was called by the Greeks and Romans the "Egyptian bean," and was regarded by those races as emblematic of Egypt. It did not differ from the ordinary lotus except in the large dimensions of the leaves and the size and loveliness of its blossoms. The leaf of the flower varied from one to one and a half feet in diameter. It had two rows of petals six inches in length, of a crimson or rose-colored purple, and inside of these was a dense fringe of stamens surrounding and protecting the ovary. The fruit developed into a sweet, wholesome nut or almond, divided into two lobes by a bitter green leaf or corculum (removed before eating), with a shell shaped like the rose of a watering pot and studded with seeds (about the size of small acorns and to the number of twenty or thirty), which projected from the upper surface in a circle about three inches in diameter. Both the nuts and roots were eaten by the poorer classes.

Wheat and barley were grown in all the provinces in the valley of the Nile, as were also, though to a lesser extent, rice, millet, pulse, peas, beans, lentils, hommos (*Cicer arietinum*), gilban (*Lathyrus sativus*), carthamus, lupins, bamia, jigl (*Raphanus sativus*—Linn., Herodot., Pliny), simsin, indigo, cassia, senna, colocynth, cummin (the seeds of which were used for bread), durrha, coriander, cucurbitae, onions, cucumbers, leeks, etc.

The onions were mild and of an excellent flavor. Nicerates quotes Homer as authority for the statement that they were much relished when eaten with wine.

According to Diodorus, children and even some grown persons lived at that time solely on roots and esculent herbs, eating them both raw and cooked.

The bread or cake used in the homes of the wealthy was made from wheaten flour; those one degree lower in the social scale made use of barley meal, and the poorer classes ate bread of the durrha (Holcus sorghum) flour.

GREECE BEFORE THE AGE OF LUXURY

It is impossible within these pages to tabulate with absolute correctness any hard and fast menu as the diet of the ancient Greeks, as it varied greatly according to the products of the several parts of the diversified country over which they ruled, but one can by the process of elimination arrive at fairly satisfactory generalities.

The principal food of the poorer classes was bread. It was not a very appetizing kind, however, as it usually consisted of a simple dough of barley meal moistened with water, or, occasionally, poor wine. It was eaten without cooking or any further preparation. This was the universal food of the Spartans.

The middle and wealthy classes partook, though, of baked wheaten bread, which was called by Homer "the strength of life."

All other kinds of food, with the exception of sweet cakes, cheese and a few vegetables and fruits, were at first considered (save by the inhabitants of the cities) as luxuries—somewhat as even now amongst old-fashioned people in Scotland, the term "kitchen" is applied to all edible articles other than dry bread.

Of sweet cakes there were many kinds. They were flavored with various seeds and sweetened with honey. Sugar, though, if known at all, was used only for its medicinal properties.

Cheese was eaten mixed with wine or honey and salt.

Dried figs and grapes were much liked, especially by the Athenians, and olives were even then pickled for a relish.

The vegetables that were formerly cultivated are not easily distinguished by the names applied to them by different writers, but it is certain that lettuce, cabbage, peas, beans, vetches, leeks, onions, parsley and thyme were grown, as well as truffles and mushrooms. Vegetables were eaten in the form of soup, served on hot dishes with sauce or dressed as salad.

In the numerous towns large quantities of fish were sold. The salt water were more generally preferred than the fresh water varieties, although especial favor was bestowed on the eels that were obtained from Lake Copais in Boeotia. There grew up early in history a heavy trade in fish from the Black Sea and even from the coasts of Spain.

Although frequent mention is made of fish, cheese and vegetable markets, a meat market seems to have been almost unknown. From this and also from the fact that the word which designated butchers' meat also signified "victim," it may be concluded that oxen were primarily slaughtered only at sacrificial feasts.

The flesh of the hare was more highly esteemed than that of any other kind of four-footed game. Of wild birds the thrush was most relished.

Pheasants and woodcock were plentiful, and quails were made to act as combatants for the edification of the Grecian youth.

Domestic fowls and eggs were common.

Butter was seldom made, as it was considered unwholesome, olive oil (as at the present time) being used in its place.

Although the Greeks were fond of water as a beverage, the difficulty of obtaining it of good quality, combined with the tremendous production of wine, made the latter the national drink. It was, however, seldom drank in an undiluted condition, and the Northerners, who were in the habit of drinking it neat, were denounced as unappreciative barbarians. But this is not very strange, as the large amount of fir resin which is still added to most Greek wines, makes them too strong and bitter for the civilized palate to drink unless tempered by water.

The first juice extracted from the press before treading was set apart as choice wine, the pressed grapes being then used for the making of the commoner variety or vinegar.

The wine was often boiled and mixed with salt for exportation, and aromatic herbs and berries were added to impart different flavors. It was then placed in earthenware jars sealed with pitch.

The various kinds may be roughly classed by colors. The black was the strongest and sweetest; the white was the weakest, and that of golden color was dry and very fine in flavor.

The wines grown in the districts of Lesbos, Chios, Sikyon, and Phlios were the most esteemed. Age was considered when estimating the value of wine, but the preference for any special year of vintage seems to have been unknown.

Even in those early days epicures whenever possible cooled their jars with snow before pouring out the wine.

Cow's milk was not liked, but the first milk of goats and sheep was often drank, although more generally used for the manufacture of cheese.

The morning meal seldom consisted of more than bread dipped in wine and water, resembling closely the morning coffee of the

Continent. The principal meal of the very early Grecians, as in the case of nearly all young nations, was served about noon, but as civilization advanced, the hour grew later, until 5 o'clock became most popular, a light luncheon then being served in the middle of the day.

Although Homer represents his chiefs as being always ready to sit down and gorge themselves with meat, the Grecian gentleman was not a disciple of "high living" or indolence. He desired and appreciated the charm of sober conversation and intellectual stimulus. Homer recognized this when he said, "Nor did the mind of any stand in want of an equal feast."

The social instincts and the warmth of feeling amongst the Hellenic race made dinners and festival events of every day occurrence, and caused them to fill a prominent part in the lives of all, but the diet of the Homeric age was wonderfully simple (in those early days the most elaborate dinners consisted of only two courses—the first of meat, usually roasted sheep, oxen or pigs, and vegetables; the second of cakes, sweetened with the honey of Hymettus, and dried and fresh fruits), for appetites were held subordinate to the love of music and the dance.

> "* * * Nor can I deem
> Aught more delightful than the general joy
> Of a whole people, when the assembled guests,
> Seated in order in the royal hall,
> Are listening to the minstrel, while the board
> Is spread with bread and meats, and from the jars
> The cup-bearer draws wine and fills the cups.
> To me there is no more delightful sight."
> (Plato.)

Invitations were generally given a few days in advance by the host in person in the market or any other place of common sojourn.

Unlike the Egyptians, the Grecians made their toilets and anointed themselves before arriving at their host's house.

But before eating,

"* * * In a bowl
Of silver, from a shapely ewer of gold,
A maid poured water o'er the hands and set
A polished table near them."

Then, if any had traveled from a distance, their feet were bathed in perfumed water and wine.

Meanwhile the male attendants were not idle—

"* * * Some in the bowls
Tempered the wine with water, some cleansed
The table with light sponges and set
The banquet forth and carved the meats for all."

A separate table was in those days usually provided for each guest, though the rule was not strictly observed.

In some cases, diners-out were accompanied and attended by their own servants. In a few districts in modern Greece this is still habitual.

Chairs and stools were generally used as seats, the custom of reclining on couches not being introduced until a later date.

As napkins were then unknown, the guests wiped their fingers on towels and in pieces of specially prepared dough, which were thrown under the table after being used.

There were spoons (of metal, often of gold — Athenaeus), but hollow pieces of bread were generally used in their stead.

The carver presided at a table and cut the meats into small pieces, as individual forks and knives were then unknown. The portions were usually of uniform size, although any very honored person was presented with larger or choicer morsels.

The diluted wine was then transferred by ladles to the drinking cups or beakers, to be distributed by boy servants. The first cup was handed from one to another of the guests untouched as a sort of salutation.

It was not customary to drink before the meal had been served.

Bread was handed round in little baskets woven from slips of ivory.

Moderation was universally observed. It was deemed gluttonous to linger long over a repast, and contemptible to imbibe too freely of wine.

> "* * * When the calls of thirst
> And hunger were appeased, the diners thought
> Of other things that well become a feast.
> Song and the dance."

But here again all ribaldry was debarred. Tender hymns and rhapsodies were sung to the accompaniment of the harp by trained singers, who were seated at special tables on silver-mounted thrones.

Games of various kinds usually followed, and with conversation filled out the time until the gathering dispersed.

House picnics were much in vogue:

"* * * * Meantime came
Those who prepared the banquets to the halls
Of the great monarch. Bringing sheep And strengthening
wine they came. Their wives, who on their brows
Wore snowy fillets, brought the bread, and thus
Within the halls of Menelaus all
Was bustle setting forth the evening meal."

Among the dining room utensils should be mentioned the various baskets of copper, silver, gold and ivory wire; vessels for mixing wine, usually of silver, but sometimes of the more precious metal, and cups of elaborate design and costly workmanship.

Drinking vessels: Bowls, beakers and rhyta

The cups were of various shapes and sizes. The "depas" had two handles and was made of wood, thickly covered with gold studs. Another, the "kypellon," was broad and shallow, made of various metals, usually gold. The "phiate" was very similar in appearance to the kypellon. The "kotyle" was so small as to

38

merely hold "a scanty draught, which only wet the lips, but not the palate."

The "sykphos" and "kissybion" were simple wooden cups in use amongst the peasantry. They were usually made of the wood of the cypress.

Skilled cooks were seldom regularly employed on the domestic staff. They usually congregated in the market places and when any particular occasion necessitated their services they were hired by the day. As also nowadays they generally represented several nations, and they gained in social importance as the love of luxury gradually overcame the custom of simple fare.

The regular staff of household servants, slaves in fact, were under the management of a general steward, himself a slave, who attended personally to the buying and superintended the details of all the other departments.

Wine jugs or oinochoai

But besides these private dinners, occasion often brought about banquets on a much larger scale, sometimes in honor of religion or of death.

"* * * There upon the ocean's side
They found the people offering coal black steers
To dark haired Neptune. On nine seats they sat,
Five hundred on each seat; nine steers were slain
For each five hundred there."

There was also a great difference between the foods of the ordinary people and that of the heroes described in the classics. According to Homer, who was probably guilty of exaggeration, the athletes consumed enormous quantities of various meats (roasted or broiled, by the way—never boiled), which comprised their entire diet with the exception of wine and bread. Beef, mutton, venison, and especially pork, were mentioned.

"He spake and girt his tunic round his loins
And hastened to the sties in which the herds
Of swine were lying. Thence he took out two
And slaughtered them and scraped them, sliced the flesh
And fried it upon spits and when the whole
Was roasted, brought and placed it reeking hot,
Still in the spits and sprinkled with white meal."

Fish and cheese were only considered worthy of the athletic when animal flesh was scarce. Nor were these giants possessed of very fastidious palates.

"* * * * At the fire
Already lie the paunches of two goats
Preparing for our evening meal, and both
Are filled with fat and blood."
"* * * * As one turns and turns
The stomach of a bullock filled with fat

> And blood before a fiercely blazing fire
> And wishes it were done * * * *."

The hospitality of the early Grecians was unbounded. The high moral and social standard of the masses of the people rendered it possible to extend greater courtesy towards strangers than would have been deemed prudent in later days. Every stranger or traveller who knocked at the door of a residence was sure of a welcome. No questions were asked him until he had been generously entertained in every feasible manner, for he stood under the protection of Zeus Xenios, guardian of the guest.

This lavish friendliness was probably caused by, or was perhaps itself the cause of, the scarcity of hostelries of reputable character. A spirit of compassion also existed, as it was then considered an ill fortune that made one journey far from home.

As the centuries of increasing wealth and power relaxed the rigidity of the morals of these ancient inhabitants of Greece, the love of luxury gradually supplanted the absorbing desire for intellectual enjoyment which had at first raised them so far above the people of the neighboring territories. Gluttonous devotion to the table, in conjunction with numerous vices, undermined the physical as well as the moral constitution, and the country which had astounded the ages with the valor of its sons, which had proved invulnerable to numerous martial forces, succumbed to the influence of sensual tastes and passions, suggested by the idleness of worldly success. And as their worship of their palates grew, the trained cook obtained an even greater influence until his position became one of extreme importance, and was so recorded by the poets and dramatists of the time.

Little difference, in fact, was there between the habits of the latter day Greeks and the Romans in the days of their great wealth, for Grecian luxuries and Grecian habits were the models that Rome took as its models, so we will pass on to the next chapter, inferentially describing the former while depicting the latter.

ROME IN THE DAYS OF HER GREATEST PROSPERITY

The food of the early Romans resembled to a great extent that of the Greek heroes (their national dish was pulmentarium, a porridge made of pulse), but to avoid repetitions we will pass over the first centuries of Roman history, choosing as our subject Rome in the days of prosperity.

It should, however, be mentioned that Greece never attained such enormous wealth as Rome, and that even in her greatest recklessness she was more refined. Goethe said that in the days of their highest civilization the Romans remained parvenus; that they did not know how to live, that they wasted their riches in tasteless extravagance and vulgar ostentation—but it must be remembered that, whereas the civilization of the nineteenth century is industrial, that of Rome was militant, and to that should be attributed the fact that some of the simplest means of comfort were then unknown.

Many moderns are inclined to doubt the assertions made concerning the countless riches and marvellous expenditures of those days. They read with skepticism the writings of Juvenal, Seneca and the elder Pliny. But, though in some cases exaggeration was doubtless resorted to, sufficient proof remains to convince the observing mind that the wealth of the Roman far surpassed the wildest dreams of the richest man of the present day. The ruins of the Colosseum and of the baths of Caracalla, two structures raised solely for pleasure, impress us with their stupendous magnificence, and even the twentieth century has failed to equal the palaces of the nobles.

Moreover, it must be remembered that the wealthy Roman owned many mansions. Each of the larger ones was a miniature city, sheltering a small army of slaves. The buildings were surrounded by parks, vineyards, woods and artificial lakes. The atria and peristyles were embellished with valuable paintings and statues. The walls and ceilings of the chambers were decorated with gold and precious stones. Nowhere else, recorded in the history of the world, with the possible exception of the palaces of the Incas, has gold ever been so lavishly used. On the furniture and ornaments alone, millions were expended. A single cup of murra brought 1,000,000 sesterces ($40,000). A small citrus wood table cost a similar sum—yet Seneca owned 500 of them, an outlay on that class of furniture alone of $20,000,000.

All Italy was covered with the country residences of the patricians. They were found in numbers on the coast of Campania, the Sabine hills and the lakes of the North.

The most esteemed members of the household staff were the coqui (cooks) and the pistores (fancy bakers). They often amassed large fortunes from their salaries and the many presents they received. All the other servants (who were usually slaves) were under the jurisdiction of a headman, an *atriensis*.

The first meal (*ientaculum*) was light, consisting ordinarily of bread and wine with honey, dates, olives or cheese. At the prandium (their *déjeuner à la fourchette*, which took the place of their noon dinner of former days), meats, vegetables, fruits, bread and wine were provided. After the second meal, the meridiato (or in modern language, the siesta) was enjoyed, as it is in the Italy of this century—although, unlike the sleepy town we know, business Rome then never slept.

After the short midday rest came games and exercises. The youth betook themselves to Campus Martius. The older members of the family made use of the sphaeristerium, a private gymnasium and ball room, which was found in every house. With it were connected the private baths.

The cena, the principal meal, commenced at 3, 4 or 5 o'clock in the afternoon. Seldom less than four hours were spent at table. Pliny, the elder, who was considered a very abstemious man, sat down to his meal at 4 o'clock, and remained there "until it began to grow dark in summer and soon after night in winter," at least three hours. The amount of food consumed would be incredible were it not for the explanation recorded by Seneca, "Edunt ut vomant; vomant ut edunt."

The dinner menu given below was of a very ordinary affair:

Gustus.
Sorrel Lettuce
Pickled Cabbage and Gherkins
Radishes, Mushrooms, etc.   Oysters
Sardines   Eggs
First Course.
Conger Eels   Oysters   Two kinds of Mussels
Thrushes on Asparagus   Fat Fowls
Ragout of Oysters and other Shellfish with black and white
Maroons.
Second Course.
Shellfish and other Marine Products
Beccaficos   Haunches of Venison Wild Boar
Pastry of Beccaficos and other Birds.

45

Third Course.

Sow's Udder	Boar's Head
Fricassee of Fish	Fricassee of Sow's Udders
Various kinds of ducks	Roast Fowl
Hares Sausages	Roast Pig

Peacocks

Fourth Course.

Pastry in wonderfully elaborate forms and colors

Pirentine bread

Fifth Course.

Fruits and wines.

The "gustus," or appetizer, was also variously known as the "gustatio." A favorite drink served with it was a mulsum of Hymetian honey and Falernian wine.

Toothpicks made from the leaves of the mastich pistachio were in common use.

All the dishes were carved at the sideboards by expert carvers who were trained in schools by practice on jointed wooden models.

Salt was much used in the flavoring of dishes and also to mingle with sacrifices.

Fowls were fattened in the dark. Ducks and geese were fed on figs and dates. Pigs were cooked in fifty different ways. Boars were cooked whole; peacocks with their tails. Sausages were imported from Gaul.

Vitellius and Apicius feasted on the tongues of flamingoes, and Elagabalus on their brains.

The greater the waste at a dinner, the more absurd the

extravagance, the more successful it was deemed. This idea was carried out in every department. A mullet of ordinary size was cheap—one that was rather heavy easily brought 6,000 sesterces ($240.00).

A Roman bakery

Frame work of a Roman dining couch

In order to lengthen the time, jugglers, rope-dancers, buffoons and actors were introduced between courses. Beautiful Andalusian girls charmed the dinners with their voluptuous dances. Even gladiators were engaged. Games of chance concluded the entertainment when the condition of the revellers permitted.

At any large affair, an archon, or toastmaster, was selected by ballot or acclamation. His duty it was to regulate the proportions of water and wine and the size of the cups in which it was served. It was usual to commence with the smallest and end with the largest.

At the table, the somber togas were exchanged for gay-colored garments (*syntheses*), and the shoes for sandals. Some of the more ostentatious changed their costumes several times during the progress of a meal. The head and breast were sometimes wreathed with flowers and ornaments.

The tables first used were of quadrangular shape—three sides being decorated for the guests and the fourth left vacant to facilitate the movements of the attendants. They, however, were soon supplanted by small tables of marble, bronze or citrus. These and a large sideboard supported an amount of heavy gold and silver utensils.

The diners reclined on costly sofas, inlaid with tortoise shells and jewels, and the lower parts decked with embroidered gold. The pillows were stuffed with wool and covered with gorgeous purple. The cushions which supported the elbows were covered with silk stuffs, often marked to designate the places of the various guests.

48

Three people occupied each sofa. The lowest place on the middle sofa was the seat of honor.

The room or hall was illuminated by lamps and candles, set on individual and very expensive stands or massed in candelabras of great magnificence. The oils and fats used for illumination were diluted with substances which under the influence of heat gave forth odors of great fragrance.

Each guest brought his own napkin.

Ivory-handled knives were manufactured, but seldom used, as the reclining position rendered the spoons (*ligulae*) more convenient.

The dessert was arranged on the sideboards under the supervision of the pistor and structor before the meal commenced.

A nomenclator was the regular employe of every patrician. His sole office was to prompt his master on the names of his guests and clients, or hangers-on.

Much care was devoted by the wealthy to their private stores of wines. They were sealed in jars or bottles of baked clay, with labels attached bearing the year of the consulship during which they were made. Some old wines were very expensive. That of Campania was considered the best. The Caecuban Falernian was very good. He was pitied who was forced to drink the Vatican!

Greek wines were popular and were found in many Roman cellars.

In winter, wine was heated with water, honey and spices in a caldarium, a vessel fitted with a small charcoal furnace, closely resembling the Russian samovar.

A banquet in the days of ancient Rome (original taken from a stone carving excavated from the site of Pompeii)

Being unable to sensibly decrease their riches by ordinary methods, many novel ideas were put in use, often at great expense.

Nero constructed in his golden house a vaulted ceiling which turned continuously on its axis.

At a banquet given by Otho, tubes of gold and silver suddenly protruded from various parts of the hall and sprinkled perfumes on the assembly.

Petronius describes a rather fanciful affair given by Trimalchio.

After the company had taken their places and young Egyptian slave girls had bathed their hands and feet in scented snow water, there was placed on the table a gold salver, inlaid with tortoise shell, in the middle of which stood an ass of bronze bearing silver panniers, one filled with white and the other with black olives. On his back sat a Silenus pouring from a wineskin the favorite sauce the *garum*; at one side were sausages on a silver gridiron, under which were plums and red pomegranate kernels to represent glowing coals, and placed around were trays bearing vegetables, snails, oysters and other appetizers.

When that course had been removed, another dish was brought in, of which the central feature was a hen of carved citrus wood with expanded wings, brooding over a nest of peafowls' eggs. These eggs were handed around on silver egg-spoons weighing each more than half a pound. When the shells were broken, some of the guests were horrified to find within them half-hatched chicks; but on closer inspection these proved to be beccaficos cooked in egg sauce.

As the plates were being removed, a chorus of Oriental beauties chanted their strange songs. A slave by accident let fall a silver dish; he stooped to pick it up—the atriensis boxed his ears and bade him sweep it out with the other fragments.

Wine of rare virtue and great age was then brought in and distributed with almost obtrusive extravagance.

The first heavy course again surprised many of those who were present. It consisted apparently of the most ordinary dishes and joints. But these proved to be merely cleverly designed covers, which on being lifted, disclosed roasted pigs, field fares, capons, noble bartels and turbots. In the centre was a plump hare which, by the addition of a pair of wings, had been made to resemble a Pegasus. The carving was done in the presence of the diners and to the strains of slow music.

Next came a huge boar roasted whole, with two palm twig baskets filled with dates, hanging from his tusks. By his side were eight small pigs, cleverly molded in paste, which were presented to guests as remembrances of the occasion.

Following the boar was a large swine, also cooked whole. After much acclamation, the carver was about to do his work, when with a look of disgust he announced that it had not been disemboweled. The cook was called and severely chided. He feigned regret and made many excuses; then seizing a heavy knife, ripped the animal open, letting fall into the dish a mass of sausages and rich puddings.

After the pig had been carried away and while the dessert was being placed on the table, the ceiling opened and a silver hoop descended bearing gold, silver and alabaster phials of essences, silver and jewel coronets and many other things of similar character.

The pastry had been made to resemble shellfish, field fares, etc. Quinces were stuck full of almonds to imitate sea urchins.

Surrounded by flowers was a figure of Vertumnus, with its bosom piled with fruits. The guests were invited to help themselves, and the pressure of their hands on the fruit caused a shower of the daintiest perfume.

When all had partaken to repletion of the goods served, the spirit of Bacchus was given full sway, half nude dancers and singers threw off all restraint, and there were enacted scenes of riotous carousing for which Rome in its decadence became notorious.

A weird dinner was once given by the Emperor Domitian. He invited a number of senators and knights to dine with him at a late hour. When they arrived they found that the banquet room had been draped in somber black. At each seat had been placed a tombstone bearing the inscription of a diner and naked black slaves danced weird dances and served up funeral viands on black dishes. When the company had been dismissed, its members found that all their slaves had disappeared and unknown bearers carried them to their homes. Each found on his return a message and a souvenir awaiting him—a silver tombstone bearing his name.

Readers will find recorded in this chapter many things which are matters of general knowledge, but this, they will readily understand, is unavoidable when treating on the customs of so well known a people as the Jews and drawing on the Bible for much of the information given. As the facts drawn from the Scriptures have though been supplemented by the results of the researches of many eminent travelers and writers, it is hoped that the combination will be found worthy of the time expended on its perusal.

The Mosaic dietary laws which for more than three thousand years formed the text of important social and religious observances among the inhabitants of the chosen kingdom were the outcome of a comparison of the regulations and practices of contemporary nations. Whether the system was compiled in the interest of humanity or health, it remains true that it has proved itself to be one of the best economic regimes ever made public. If for no other reason, the life of the ancient Jew is especially interesting to those who study the foods of men, past and present—although it must be admitted that the precepts they compiled were more conducive to sound digestion than some of the practices they followed!

The diet of the ancient Jews consisted at first, as did that of all the pioneers of the human race, of but a few articles of food. But, though meat was not consumed in large quantities, writers err when they describe the food of Orientals as being light and simple. Orientals did, and do, make use of an inordinate amount of grease in cooking. Eggs and rice were, whenever circumstances permitted, saturated with fat or oil and meats and vegetables were frequently simmered in fat before being stewed. It was not unusual for a family of six or seven persons to consume an average of two hundred pounds a year, and some of their compounds would have ill suited delicate stomachs.

Bread, as in all ancient countries, constituted the greater part of the food of the middle and lower classes. In Leviticus, Psalms and Ezekiel, reference is made to the "staff of bread." It was most generally eaten after being dipped into cheap wine or weak gravy.

The fresh green ears of wheat were often eaten without cooking, the husks being rubbed off by hand. The grain was, though, more usually roasted in a pan after being carefully sorted over, and it was sometimes bruised and dried in the sun, to be afterwards served with oil.

"Kibbe" was a mixture composed of cracked wheat, boiled and dried, beaten up with meat, onions, spices and the nut of a species of pine.

Wheat was also ground by women in hand mills formed of two stones, the under one fixed and the upper movable.

The middle classes ate meat, vegetables, fruit or fish also, but always as supplementary dishes to the staple article, bread.

Although in the earliest days the mistress and daughters of the house did the baking, female servants were later employed by the wealthier families. In Jerusalem indeed professional bakers,

55

men, became so numerous that a section of the town bore the title of "Bakers' Street."

The flour used in the manufacture of the common bread was mixed with water or milk and kneaded with the hands in a small wooden bowl or trough. Except in cases of great haste, leavening was then added. The dough was allowed to stand for several hours, sometimes for the whole night, in moderate heat. It was next rolled out and cut into circular pieces about eight inches in diameter and three-quarters of an inch in thickness. These were occasionally punctured and soaked with oil.

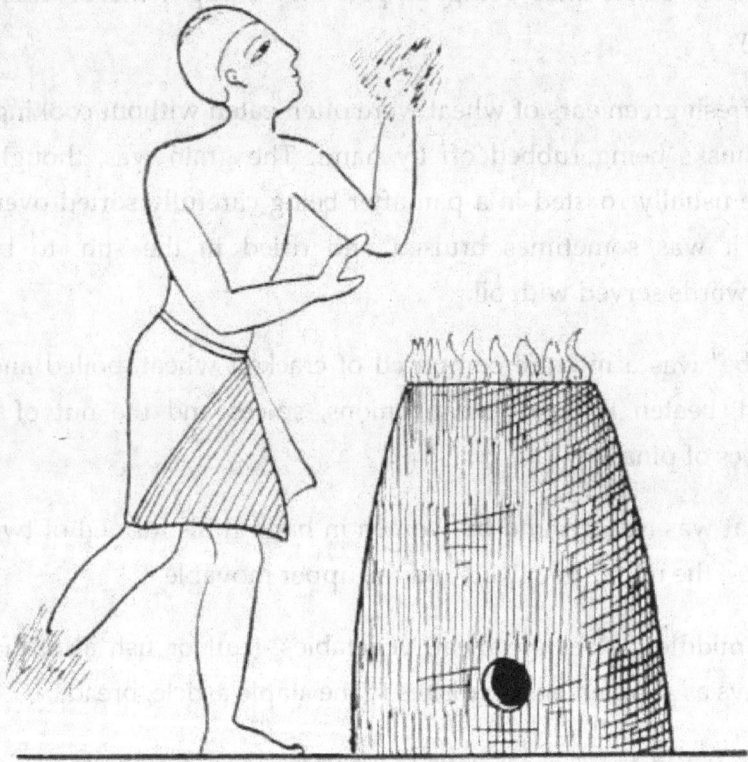

A portable oven of the Jews and Egyptians
(From an old Egyptian drawing)

A more delicate kind of bread was twice kneaded before baking, and stimulating seeds were added to it. Various varieties of thin cakes were also baked every day and biscuits of substantial character were furnished for travelers.

The professional bakers did their work in fixed, specially constructed ovens, but portable ovens were usually found in private houses. They were in the shape of stone or metal jars about three feet in height, and were heated from the interior with wood, dried grass or flower stalks, the cakes being placed on the ashes or the exterior sides of the oven after the fire had burned down.

In other cases, a hole dug in the ground formed the oven, the sides being covered with clay and the bottom with pebbles. Again, sometimes the cakes were cooked on heated stones or by the more primitive method of laying them directly on burning logs, or between two layers of dried dung (then lighted and burned).

Some also baked the cakes in pans with oil and ate them whilst hot with honey, or cooked them in such thin layers that they crumbled in the fingers.

Figs were eaten fresh and dried. Pomegranates, mulberries, sycamore figs, citrons and apples were widely cultivated. Grapes were eaten raw or made into fruit cake (which possessed distinctly stimulating qualities). Similar cakes were also made of raisins, dates and figs—which were compressed into bricks, and when hardened could be cut up only by the use of an axe!

The bunches of grapes often attained a weight of twelve pounds.

Walnuts were plentiful. Oranges were introduced at a later date.

Among the vegetables grown were lentils (which were boiled and eaten with butter oil or fat and pepper), leeks, onions, beans, barley, lettuce, endive, purslane and other herbs. Vegetables were usually boiled as potage.

The spices most in favor were cummin, dill, coriander, mint, mustard and salt. Cummin was threshed with a rod and with salt served as a sauce.

Pistachio nuts and almonds were popular as whets.

Salads were extensively known.

Honey was used in some cakes as a substitute for sugar. It was also eaten raw or with other articles of food, even fish.

Various artificial productions made from fruits and the exudations of trees and shrubs bore the title of honey, the best known of which was the boiled down juice of the grape, then called "d'bash," known to modern Arabs as "dibs."

"Butter and honey" and "milk and honey" are in Biblical language synonyms of the diet of prosperity.

The butter then used differed from our own product inasmuch as the hot sun to which the cream was exposed when being churned rendered the completed article more liquid. Even to-day in some parts of the Orient the butter served to visiting Europeans has to be manufactured especially for them from cold cream.

Cheese consisted of coagulated buttermilk, dried until hard and then ground.

Oil was made from various vegetables, but that of the olive was most esteemed.

Wine and water were carried in vessels made of the skins of goats, kids or other clean animals. After the animal had been killed, the head, feet and tail were cut off and the body was drawn out of the skin, which was then tanned (acacia bark being sometimes called into service). The hairy part of the skin formed the exterior of the vessel, the legs and the end of the tail being sewn up. When filled, the neck was tied up.

An ox skin was used to make a "gerba" which formed a storage chamber for large quantities of liquor. One of average size contained sixty gallons.

The milk of cows, sheep, camels and goats was drank. When fresh it was known as "khalab," when sour as "khema." The latter was used in the composition of salads and for cooking meats, etc.

A strengthening beverage was made by heating milk over a slow fire and then adding a small piece of old khema or other acid to make it coagulate. Much of this was bottled and kept for future use. It was the universal refreshment offered strangers and the ancient Jew, like the modern Arab, refused to accept payment for it.

The other drinks of the people were barley water; sherbet (made by partially dissolving fig cake in water); pomegranate wine; beer made from barley with herbs such as the lupin and skirret; honey, date, fig, millet and grape wines and a drink made by placing raisins in jars of water and burying them until fermentation had taken place. Water was imbibed in large quantities after meals.

Vinegar was made by mixing barley with wine, or soured wine was used.

The prohibition expressed in the ninth chapter of Genesis against animal blood as an article of diet was repeated with detailed instructions in Leviticus. Instead of devoting a large amount of space to recounting the regulations there expressed, it will perhaps be better to make only a general classification of them.

There were interdicted: *Sheretz haaretz*, creeping things; *sheretz haof*, winged insects, with the exception of the fully developed locust; of *sheretz hamayim*, creatures dwelling in water, those which were not provided with fins and scales; of the feathered species those which were not furnished by nature with the implements with which to clean themselves; of the quadrupeds and animals of the chase those that did not chew the cud or were not provided with split hoofs.

The fat parts of animals were also reserved for the altar and temple offerings.

Special interdictions were announced against dead or injured animals; though these did not extend to strangers. In the New Testament, these laws are also mentioned as applying to healthy animals that had been strangled or killed in any manner other than that prescribed.

In a word, the Mosaic laws prohibited the use of any flesh that was diseased, bruised or rendered unwholesome by the presence of too much blood and also of the flesh of animals that were not cleanly in habits, diet or body.

Oxen were not eaten when older than three years.

It is not necessary to give here the oft-repeated methods of Jewish butchery, as they have been of late so frequently described—and highly endorsed—by medical and scientific men.

Fresh fish (eaten generally broiled) appears to have been the principal article of diet in the environs of the Sea of Galilee. The Jews, however, were not well versed in the character of the different species. They roughly classed them as big, small, clean and unclean.

Salt fish also was imported into Jerusalem.

Locusts were considered to be but meagre fare, but they were eaten salted, dried and roasted with butter in a pan.

An ordinary kitchen was equipped with a range, a heavy caldron, a large fork or flesh hook, a wide, open metal vessel for heating water, etc., two or more earthenware pots and numerous dishes.

The kid, lamb or calf, killed on the advent of a holiday or in honor of a guest, would sometimes be roasted or baked whole, but it was usually cut up and boiled in a caldron filled with water or milk and set over a wood fire, the scum being taken off from time to time and salt and spices added.

The meat and broth were served up separately or together as desire might dictate.

The principal meal was held in the early evening, although occasionally noon was chosen for a big banquet.

The early Hebrews seated themselves on the ground when partaking of a meal; but their descendants soon succumbed to the example of the Egyptians and adopted the reclining couch, which was universally used in the time of Christ.

The first reference we have to the change in custom is found in the book of Amos, where the prophet rebukes those who "lie upon beds of ivory." Ezekiel also inveighs against one who "sat on a stately bed with a table prepared before it."

Each couch seated from three to five persons, and the women usually dined with the men.

The meat and vegetables were sometimes served in one large dish, into which each in turn dipped his bread, but on other occasions portions were placed on individual plates.

Many events were made excuses for festivals.

The "mishteh" was a drinking party, which in the apostolic age was called a "komos" and was often the occasion of gross licentiousness.

The cups used were modelled after those made by the Egyptians. The "cup bearer" or butler held a very important position in a rich man's household.

During times of fasting or sorrow, all meats, wines, etc., were eschewed. They were called the "bread of desires."

Prison fare consisted of bread or pulse and water.

The vine or apples of Sodom, the "Dead Sea fruits that tempt the eye, but turn to ashes on the lips" of which Josephus wrote and Moore and Byron sang, are worthy of more than passing notice. They have caused a great deal of discussion among scientists and travelers who have differed in their opinions as to the identity of the fruit or plant mentioned.

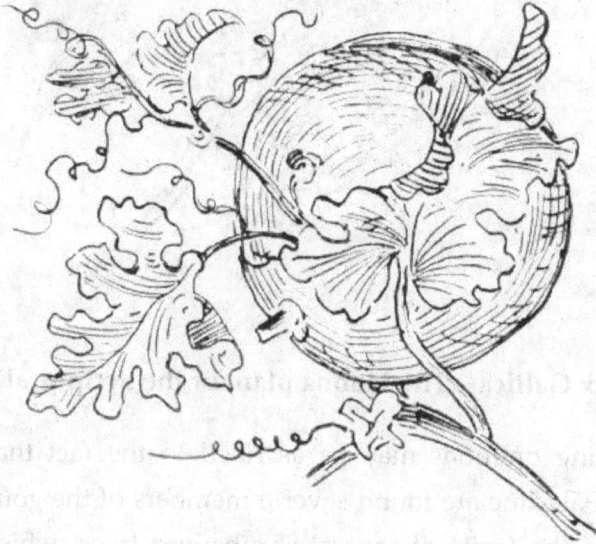

The colocynth—"the Dead Sea fruits"

As the *ecbalium elaterium*, with variations in name, it has been described by Dioscorides, Theophrastus, Pliny, Celeius, Rosenmuller, Winner and Gesenius; as the *cucumbis prophetarium*, and *solanium sodomaeum* by others; as the *asclepias procera* by Burckhardt, Irby, Mangles and Dr. Robinson. Among still other disputing writers may be mentioned Pococke, Hasselquist, Seetzen, Elliot and Chateaubriand.

Michaelis, Oedman, Dr. J. D. Hooker and the Rev. W. Houghton agree that Josephus referred to the fruit of the colocynth (*citrullus colocynthis*) which resembles an orange in appearance, and when dry will burst on pressure with a crashing noise.

Tamarix Gallica—The Manna plant of the Scriptural desert

The varying opinions may be ascribed to the fact that in the south of Palestine are found several members of the gourd tribe, as well as the fruits of several shrubs and trees, which under certain conditions answer very closely to the descriptions afforded us of the "Dead Sea Fruits," although the colocynth is the only one that answers them in every way.

The palm tree, once so plentiful in Judaea, is now rare and in the vicinity of Jericho is extinct, the last one having died a few years ago.

All readers of the Scriptures remember the important part which manna played in the history of the Jews. The manna which is at the present day known in the Arabian desert through which the Israelites passed is collected in June from the tarfa or tamarisk shrub (*Tamarix Gallica*). According to Burkhardt, it drops from the thorns on to the sticks and leaves which cover the ground and must be gathered early in the day or it will be melted by the heat of the sun. Its fall is said to be caused by the punctures made by insects. The Arabs cleanse, boil and strain it and put it up in leather bottles, and thus prepared it will retain its virtues for several years. It is used in the place of honey or butter—it is never eaten alone. It is abundant only in wet seasons, and in a very dry year it is not found at all. It is not exactly peculiar in character, as there are several shrubs in India and Syria.

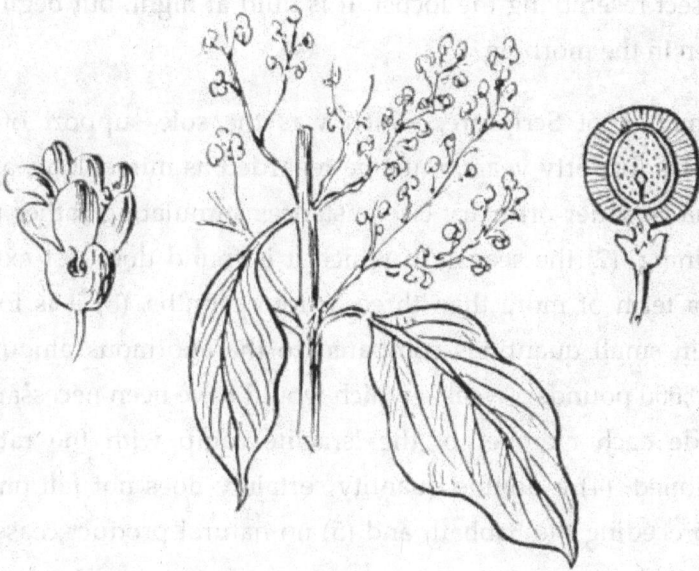

Salvadora—The arboreous Mustard Plant of Palestine

Niebuhr discovered at Mardin, in Mesopotamia, on the leaves of a tree, a species of *capparis*, a kind of manna which appears during the months of July and August, being most plentiful in wet seasons. If shaken off before sunrise, it is pure white in color. If let remain, it collects until very thick, and the leaves are then gathered and steeped in boiling water until the manna floats to the top like oil. This is called by the natives *manna essemma*, heavenly manna.

Burkhardt found in the valley of Jordan a similar gum on the leaves and branches of the tree gharrob (a species of oak), which fell to the ground in drops of brown-gray dew. Its taste at first was sweet, but after a day's exposure to the elements became acrid.

The manna of European commerce is exported from Calabria and Sicily. It drops from punctures made in a species of ash by an insect resembling the locust. It is fluid at night, but begins to harden in the morning.

The manna of Scripture, which was the sole support of the Israelites for forty years, must be regarded as miraculous, as (1) manna is under ordinary circumstances stimulating rather than sustaining, (2) the season in which it is found does not extend over a term of more than three or four months, (3) it is found only in small quantities compared to the enormous amount— 15,000,000 pounds a week—which would have been necessary to provide each member of the Israelite camp with the rations mentioned, (4) a double quantity certainly does not fall on the day preceding the Sabbath and (5) no natural product ceases at once and forever.

The mustard plant mentioned in the Gospels may have been either the common mustard plant which grows to a large size in the Orient, or it may have been the *Salvadora persica*, an arboreous plant of abundant foliage, the seeds and leaves of which have a distinct flavor of mustard.

THE CHINESE

It would be foolish to publish any strict dietary code as descriptive of the food of the people of the vast region generally known as the Chinese Empire, for apart from the difference in the products of the various sections of that diversified country, it must be remembered that the numerous tribes, which when amalgamated centuries ago formed the Empire, have retained most of their original customs, owing partly to the paucity of transportation facilities and the consequent impediments to an interchange of ideas, partly to the conservative nature of the people and partly to the influence of climate and surroundings. Furthermore, as, excepting a few fruits which are of comparatively recent introduction, such as the pineapple, the foods of Chinamen to-day closely resemble the foods of Chinamen four thousand years ago, it will not be necessary in this volume to keep very strictly apart the past and the present.

Until quite recently it was customary to regard the Chinese as uncivilized and degraded heathens who voraciously devoured all kinds of vermin and other miscellaneous tit-bits which to most people of the Western Hemisphere are repulsive even in suggestion, hence it may be well to repeat here that, although it remains true that cats, dogs and rats occasionally serve as articles of food, this happens only when provisions are scarce or among the very poor, who (as in all civilized countries), linger always on the threshold of starvation.

The Chinese, in spite of the doleful tales of some writers, are on the whole a well fed race. Beef and mutton are not plentiful except in the north, but hogs, poultry and fish, with vegetables, fruits and rice are within the reach of a majority of the population. Wrote a Chinese sage: "The scholar forsakes not his books nor the poor man his pig." Furthermore, in the preparation of their national dishes the Chinese cooks (especially those in the cities and in the households of the rich) display a high degree of skill.

Wheat, several varieties of rice and sweet potatoes are grown in all parts of the Empire, and barley, sorghum, cabbages, beans and other vegetables and sugar cane are also raised in large quantities.

Rice is seldom ground except when made into cakes.

The sorghum, or hauliang (extensively cultivated in the north), is not used as in America for the manufacture of sugar, but the seeds are ground and made into a coarse bread or used for the preparation of some brands of whiskey.

Sweet potatoes are sliced into coarse strips and dried in the sun. It is, though, considered a sign of extreme poverty to be seen eating them at any meal other than a lunch or hurried repast.

Of the vegetables, the petsae or white cabbage is the most widely cultivated.

Beans grow luxuriantly. Fully one-half of the crop is crushed for the sake of the oil, the residue being pressed into bricks and used as a fertilizer.

"Bean curds" is a very popular dish, especially for breakfast. The beans are ground to a flour, which is passed through three strainers of coarse, medium fine and very fine linen. This is boiled for an hour over a slow fire until the proper consistency is obtained.

Salted beans form quite an important article of commerce. Four catties of beans are put in a jar with one catty of salt, half a catty of ginger and a few taels of almonds and spices. The jars are then sealed and left untouched for about a month.

A more novel way is to put the beans in earthenware jars filled with very clear spring water, changing the water every four hours. In seven days tender shoots have appeared and the beans are then sold as a delicacy.

Peanuts are grown for the sake of their oil.

Hsiang-yu is a fragrant oil made from peanuts and beans, which is used for the toilet and by the poor for cooking. Castor oil answers the same purposes.

The juice of the sugar cane is extracted by crushing the stalks in two perpendicular cylinders, kept in motion by a yoke of buffalos, the juice being received in a tub placed beneath. Lime is added to the juice and it is then immediately boiled.

Within the limits of Chinese territory are found almost all known varieties of fruits, some of which are indigenous to it.

The whampee is a yellow skinned fruit about the size of a grape which hangs in clusters from the glossy-leaved trees which produce it. The flavor is tart and its three or four stones are of a greenish color.

The li-chi has a rough red exterior. Inside is a white film which incloses a watery translucent pulp of a sweetish taste and a brownish black ovoid stone.

The lo-quat is a species of medlar.

A Chinese poulterer's shop

Oranges, ginger, etc., are preserved in sugar.

Ducks are raised in almost incredible numbers. Their eggs and those of fowls are frequently hatched by artificial heat.

Eggs that have been preserved in lime for several, sometimes a great many, years are much esteemed. After a quarter of a century, the yellow assumes a dark brown color and the whites have the appearance of meat jelly—strange though it may seem, they are really excellent in that condition.

All foods served at a genuine Chinese dinner are previously cut into minute particles. The large roast pieces which adorn the tables at dinners given in seaport towns to foreigners of note are placed there merely in deference to the customs of the guests.

70

A Chinese dinner party

Rice and soup are brought on to the table in large vessels from which individual saucers are filled. Other dishes are partaken of by all present directly from the common bowl.

It is considered a token of hospitality on the part of the host or friendliness on the part of an acquaintance to take an especially choice piece of meat or vegetable from the bowl and to place it on the plate or in the mouth of a fellow diner.

The two chopsticks are both held in the right instead of separately in each hand as ordinarily believed. They are maintained by the thumb and ring finger and manipulated by the index and middle fingers. One stick remains motionless, the other is so manoeuvred as to entrap with ease a morsel of meat or even the smallest grain of rice.

The sticks (square at the top and round for the rest of their length) are made of bamboo or more precious woods, ivory or silver. On the upper portions, poems and pictures are often engraved.

Spoons are used for liquids.

Chopsticks and bowl

An ordinary meal among the middle classes consists of eight dishes—two vegetables, eggs, fish, shell fish, bird and two meats (pork and goat; or, in some parts of the north, mutton and beef).

With this will be served a large tureen of soup with rice, the latter taking the place of bread.

When eating rice, the bowl is raised by the left hand to a close proximity to the mouth and the rice is rather scooped than picked up.

The importance which is attached to rice as a life-sustaining article may be judged from the exclamation of a Chinese sailor when he was informed that it was held in but secondary repute in America. Throwing up both hands with an expression in which were combined horror and pity, he cried: "Oh, the sterile region of barbarians which produces not the necessaries of life; strange that the inhabitants have not long ago died of hunger!"

Two good meals a day, the customary number, and a light luncheon, will in the average native home represent the expenditure of about ten cents in American money.

Wine is served only on special occasions.

The hotels in the large cities are distinguished by titles as in this country, though the Chinese proprietor gives freer rein to his imagination, choosing such titles as "Cum Lee" (Golden Profits), "Cut Shing" (Rank Conferring Hotel), the "Cut Sing" (Fortunate Star), etc. They are often comparatively tall structures and are usually clustered together in one quarter of the town.

A Chinese distillery

The ground floor of the ordinary hotel is reserved for the proprietor's apartments and the kitchen. The first floor contains one public and several private dining-rooms; and the second and upper floors are divided into sleeping apartments—the partitions of which are so thin that even a whispered conversation is intelligible to a party in the adjoining room.

There is not much comfort to be obtained in the villages, and the accommodations are worse in the south and central districts than in the north and Mongolia.

The country caravansary is built in the form of a quadrangle with the walls, in the North, of mud or clay.

In the one public room, the traveler perforce mingles with cattle drovers and muleteers, but the private apartments are fairly comfortable.

The stables are usually attached to the building, with large compounds for sheep or cattle. Some of the larger establishments boast separate quadrangle stables, while some of the smaller have none at all, the animals being hitched to troughs or racks in the centre of the quadrangle.

A Chinese restaurant

The beds (*cangues*) are shaped like furnaces. The occupant, protected by a thick coverlet, reclines on the top of a stratum of chunam or asphalt, with an opening similar to the door of a furnace, in one of the perpendicular sides, by means of which a small fire is in cold weather built directly beneath the bed.

The poorer travelers sleep in the public hall.

In some cities are khans which act as depots for the goods of traveling merchants, who are boarded and lodged without charge until they have disposed of their stock, the landlord then receiving a small percentage of the sales.

The proprietor of a public inn is compelled to furnish the authorities each month with a list of the persons whom he has lodged or fed, and women are not received at all in the public hotels in the South.

The restaurants in the cities are often quite large, running to two and three stories in height.

On the ground floor is the kitchen. On the first floor at the head of the first staircase is the public dining room where a good cheap meal can be obtained, and on the second and third floors are the private and more select chambers. In each room is a bill of fare.

An ordinary first class restaurant dinner comprises from ten to thirty dishes, and for any special occasion a hundred or more are often served.

Below is the menu of a dinner which, if served to eight or ten persons at a good public city restaurant, would cost about seventy-five cents per head.

75

Fried Ham   Gizzards   Grated meat Grilled
         Dried shrimps   Preserved eggs

_____

Four kinds of dried fruits
Four kinds of fresh fruits

_____

Fat duck   Shark's fins   Swallowsnest soup
                  Meats

_____

Salted chicken   Shellfish   Meats Oysters

_____

Mushroom morels (called "Ears of the Forest"). Rice of Im-
mortals (a species of mushrooms).Tender sprouts
of bamboo

_____

Fish   Meats

The diners are usually seated at square tables in groups of eight.

Chinese whiskey or wine is served in small double-handled cups, which are constantly replenished by the attendants from vessels resembling silver coffee pots. Pipes of tobacco are also passed around at intervals.

Before eating, the host or most prominent guest pours out a libation. His table companions follow his example and all bow politely to each other.

Pastry is brought on between courses. If salt, a cup of chicken broth; if sweet, almond milk is furnished with it.

No napkins are provided, pieces of coarse brown paper being used in their stead.

Chinaman spearing fresh water turtles

The last is a sort of "trial of appetite" course. It consists of large dishes—sometimes eight or ten arranged in pyramid form—and the ever forthcoming refusal to partake of it announces the termination of the meal.

The attendants then bring in towels and bowls of hot water. They immerse the towels in the water, and after wringing them out present them to the guests in the order of their importance.

On special occasions the water is scented with otto of roses.

One habit of the attendants which is especially surprising to the novice is that as their labors during the meal increase the temperature of their bodies, the waiters divest themselves of the greater part of their clothing!

One restaurant in Canton which caters for the cheaper class of trade, feeds on an average five thousand persons daily. Each patron is served with portions of regular size, and allowance is made for any pieces which he may not eat.

The tea saloons are divided into two large rooms furnished with stools and tables. Cakes, preserved fruits and tea are served. The cups are usually covered so as to prevent the aroma of the tea from evaporating.

"Dog and cat" restaurants consist of one large public apartment, with the entrance to the dining room through the kitchen.

Soup stalls are found on the street corners of the cities. They sell luncheons of fish, pork, soups, vegetables, fried locusts, etc., from one to two cents.

The oven, or, to speak more accurately, the baking apparatus, of the average establishment is somewhat singular. It consists of a furnace resembling a copper in shape, built in the center of an outhouse. The hollow part (which is shallow) is filled with charcoal. A lid, which fits the aperture, is so suspended by chains from the beams above as to be capable of elevation or depression. Upon this lid, pastry and cakes are placed and kept directly above or at any distance from the fire, according to the heat desired.

The bakers often manufacture their bread without the use of shortening of any description.

A very popular cake consists partially of mincemeat. The baker before commencing to make it, places a pile of dough on one side and opposite it a heap of mincemeat—a mixture of pork, sugar, spices, etc. He then pulls off a piece of dough, rolls it into a ball, flattens it, covers it with the meat, rolls it into a ball again, shapes it into a ring and flattens it by a stroke of the hand into a cake of definite size and thickness.

Among other dainty dishes of Chinaland are the "t'ien ya tzu," a species of delicately flavored fat duck; "feng chi," salted chicken; a dish of amber gelatine; a salad of bamboo shoots; "huo t'ui," a dainty ham of the appearance of veal; "yü ch'ih," shark's fins, and "hai li tzu," devilled oysters with mushrooms.

Other items are salted earthworms, pigeon's eggs, pounded shrimps; bird's nest soup, a gelatinous article; beches de mer (sea slugs), water beetles and silkworms, the last named fried in oil after they have made their cocoons.

A much admired soup, prepared for an imperial feast, was of blood and mare's milk.

Oysters are very cheap in winter, selling at from five to six cents per pound.

The following receipts may be of interest as literal translations from a genuine Chinese cook book:

Steamed Shark's Fins.

> Take the sun-dried shark's fins, place in a cooking pan, add wood ashes and boil in several waters. Then take out and scrape the roughness from the fins. If not clean, boil again and scrape again until clean. Then change the water and boil again. Take out and remove the flesh, keeping only the fins themselves. Boil again and put in spring water. The frequent changing of the water is

necessary to take out the lime taste. Put the fins into the soup and stew until quite tender. Dish in a bowl, placing crab meat below and a little ham on top.

Chicken with the Liquor of Fermented Rice.

Bone a chicken and steam until just right; take out and let cool, then cut into thin slices. Next, take gelatinous rice which has been fermented with yeast and water; cook this for two hours, add a little of the juice expressed from fresh ginger, soy, sesamum and oil. Mix together with peanut oil. Dish and add fragrant herbs.

Genii Ducks.

Take a fat duck; open and clean. Take two mace of salt, rub it both outside and inside and put into an earthen dish. Take one cup of fan spirits and put (the cup with the spirits) inside the duck—only the vapor of the spirits is wanted. Steam over water until quite tender, then lift out the wine cup and put the bird into a bowl.

The most common native liquor are "suee chow," a rice brandy; "shas chin," an impure alcohol made from kauliang or sorghum; "huary chin," a yellow wine made from millet, and various spirits extracted from plums, apples, pears, etc. All liquors are drunk hot, and some of them are steeped with spices or the leaves of flowers.

Although spirits are plentiful and cheap, drunkenness is rare.

Tea, of course, is consumed by all classes.

A curious custom annually observed is the propitiatory offering

80

to the God of the Kitchen, who is worshipped in all parts of China, and who is supposed to report his observations to the Pearly Emperor Supreme Ruler.

Family Offering to the Kitchen God

He is represented in each kitchen by a slip of white or red paper (changed each year as a rule) bearing his name and title and sometimes his portrait, pasted on the wall in some convenient part of the room.

Among the better classes the kitchen god is also known as the superintendent or inspector of good and evil.

On the evening of the twenty-third day of the twelfth month a special sacrifice is made in his honor by about sixty per cent. of the population. Meats, cakes, fruits and wines are offered with candles, incense, mock money, etc., and all members of the family then kneel reverently before his representation and bow their heads in homage.

On the evening of the twenty-fourth those who have not participated in the ceremonies of the previous day, make a vegetable offering in a similar manner.

A Chinese kitchen boat

Many of the wealthier classes make both offerings on the twenty-third. The poorest use only incense and candles.

The numerous sailing vessels on the rivers and lakes are as well fitted to supply the wants of the traveler as the hotels on shore.

The houseboats and some of the passenger boats rely for their meals on the kitchen boats, which are really admirably managed.

The fishing boats make use of a very primitive heating apparatus—a large boiler in an earthenware furnace set in a part of the deck, serving as the general cook book.

A great many pages might be covered by treating on the curious festivities which celebrate so many occasions, but they have been so often described in other works that a description of them here would perhaps savor too much of needless repetition.

www.ingramcontent.com/pod-product-compliance
Lightning Source LLC
Chambersburg PA
CBHW011801040426
42448CB00017B/3326